HOW TO BE

Happy

(NO FAIRY DUST OR MOONBEAMS REQUIRED)

CARA STEIN

Fire Lizard Press

Also by this Author

Getting Unstuck
Reclaim Your Love: How to Fix Your Relationship
Relax and Color

Table of Contents

How to be Happy— *Faster!*

Thanks for purchasing this book. I'm super excited for you, and I want to do everything I can to help you. That's why I've made a free workbook to go along with this book.

۶ 35-page PDF workbook, ready for you to print out and started

۶ Guiding questions to help you go deeper and apply this book to your unique situation

۶ Thought-provoking exercises to help you find happiness in your own life

It's free! You can get it here:
http://17000-days.com/how-to-be-happy-workbook/

Preface:
Who am I to tell you anything?

The short answer is: I'm someone who has learned to be happy. I don't have a whole raft of patients, research, or case studies. I'm not a psychologist. I just have the results of one experiment.

I was a very unhappy person, miserable most of the time and scared a lot, too. I felt trapped, suffocated, selfish, mean, inadequate, listless, exhausted, unable to cope, and perpetually on the verge of blowing up or freaking out. With the help of people and books, I learned a lot of things that helped me become happy and enjoy my life. I want to pass what I've learned on to you.

Just reading is not enough to make you happy—you have to take action and change your life—but I've found that understanding how it all works helps a lot in trying to do better and feel better.

Also, not all unhappiness can be cured by changing your thinking or your approach to life. If you believe you may suffer from depression, please talk to a doctor or mental health professional about whether medication could help you.

But whether you're depressed, unhappy, or just looking to get the most out of life, I think the knowledge in this book is valuable. I hope it will help you improve your life.

Introduction: Is it really ok to be happy?

If this seems like a silly question, you're ahead of the game, because a lot of people think happiness is a sign of foolishness, laziness, or selfishness. Here are some misconceptions that I've heard:

- Happiness is all plastering over reality with smiley faces and deluding yourself into believing everything is ok. You waste time and energy telling yourself stupid, untrue affirmations and believing in nonsense. I'll take truth over happiness, thank you.

- Happy people are gullible suckers who just haven't grown up yet.

- Good people work hard—they don't have time to be happy.

❧ We're not meant to be happy in this life. The more we suffer and struggle here, the more we'll be rewarded in heaven.

In short, a lot of people believe that if you're happy, you're doing it wrong. They're afraid of happiness because they think it means losing touch with reality, or being foolish, lazy, selfish, or bad. But that's not how true happiness is. It doesn't come from pretending. It doesn't come from making a lot of money, being powerful, owning a lot of things, or sitting on the beach all day eating bonbons, either. Real happiness is:

❧ Love

❧ Optimism

❧ Courage

❧ Freedom

❧ Proactivity

❧ Security

❧ Health

❧ Spirituality

❧ Altruism

❧ Perspective

❧ Humor

❧Purpose[i]

These are true virtues. I don't know any god or man who looks down on these qualities, and they are the keys to enjoying life. They can be yours—that's what this book is about.

Chapter 1:
How Happiness Works

So few people are happy. Most of the people I know are neutral or unhappy, and most of the people I meet sure don't look happy! Happy people really stand out, partly because they're so rare.

Since hardly anybody does it, it's easy to assume that being happy is complicated, or there's some secret you have to know, or maybe you have to be born with a certain gene.

While people are born with an innate level of happiness or happiness set point, and circumstances also influence how happy you are, you still have the power to make yourself happier. Surprisingly, 50% of our happiness levels come from genetics, and only 10% from circumstances, leaving 40% that we can control.[i]

Why are so many people unhappy? It's actually pretty simple. The thing that keeps most people from being happy is fear.[ii]

Think about it for a minute. Look over your life and what

feels bad in it.

Do you get the blues every Sunday night because you'll have to go to work Monday morning? That's probably because you're afraid you'll have to do a lot of stuff you don't like, or a lot of stuff you're afraid you can't do, or both. Maybe there are also unpleasant people at work and you're afraid you'll have a run-in with them.

When you sit down to do the bills, do you get a heavy knot of dread in the pit of your stomach? Chances are, you're afraid you don't have enough money to pay for everything.

When someone cuts you off in traffic, do you blow your top? Well, who wouldn't—they could have killed someone! That's fear, too—you're angry because they put you in danger.

Most unpleasant feelings boil down to fear. If you're stressed about work or money, your relationships, what people think of you, or all the things you have to do, it all comes down to fear. This is important: fear is the enemy of happiness.

How Happiness Doesn't Work

People try a lot of things in attempt to become happy. Most of them don't work, so people just try them again, harder! Here are a few:

- Getting more money or possessions

- Getting more power or status

- Pursuing indulgent pleasures

- Focusing on their weaknesses and trying to improve them

(instead of playing to their strengths)

🕊 Striving to be perfect (and accepting nothing less)

🕊 Trying to force happiness, using false affirmations or other tricks[i]

We've all heard that money can't buy happiness, but most people don't really believe it.

More money won't make me happy—are you nuts? Come on, if I hit the lotto, I could pay off all of my debt, quit my crappy job, do what I've always wanted to do, and still have plenty to give to my family and charities. You're telling me that wouldn't make me happier?

Yes. It's surprising but true. Lots of studies have been done on this. A year after winning, lottery jackpot winners are no happier than they were before they won. Amazingly, the same is true for people who are in terrible accidents and suddenly paralyzed: a year later, they're no less happy than before.[v]

Circumstances are not what makes us happy or unhappy. Think about it: if money was enough to make us happy, there should be a lot of people walking around saying, "Wow, thank God I got that last raise! Now I have enough money, and I am happy!" Yet I've never heard anyone say that. Most rich people seem to be quite unhappy, in fact. If fortune or fame worked, you would never see movie stars and rock musicians with drug problems—they'd be too happy to be interested in drugs.

Similarly, possessions do not cause happiness. If they did, wouldn't we be happy by now? I, for one, have bought a lot of awesome things, but the only ones that have made a long-term difference are the ones that are involved in *doing something*: my spinning wheel, my kayak, my convertible. The things themselves don't matter much, but doing fun things with them adds joy to my life.

Another thing that won't make you happy is whitewashing over reality and feeding yourself a lot of bogus affirmations that you know aren't true. Any philosophy that requires you to deny reality is a false path. In fact, studies have shown that insincerity is every bit as bad for your heart as anger.[v] Your body feels the tension between the truth and the way you're acting, and finds it very destructive. It's important to look for the good in a situation, but it's even more important to be real.

These are all traps, but they're very easy to fall into, especially with media and advertisers giving us a push every chance they get! In case you don't already know, the main purpose of television, magazines, newspapers, and all popular media is to sell advertisements. That's how they make money. They produce content to get your attention so you'll see as many of their ads as possible.

Meanwhile, the advertisers' goal is to get you to buy products. This is obvious enough; the insidious part is that if you're generally content with your life, you won't feel compelled to buy much. To get you to buy, advertisers intentionally do everything they can to convince you that something is missing in your life, and if you were just prettier, had whiter teeth, used a different laundry detergent, or whatever, then people would like you better. They try to convince you that something is wrong in your life now, but if you buy their product, it will fix it, and then you'll be happy.

They get you coming and going: they tell you you're inadequate and shouldn't be happy, and then they give you a solution that will never make you happy. The more you watch or listen, the harder it is to be happy. These messages make a difference, so protect yourself from them as much as you can. Use an ad blocker on your web browser. If you listen to commercial radio, switch stations when the commercials come on. If you watch tv, at least mute the commercials, or better, watch a recording and skip past them. Better still, stop watching tv. Most of the shows are also designed to make you unhappy so you'll buy more of the advertisers' products.

If this all sounds too hard, just try it for a week and see if you feel more peaceful and content. It's much easier to be happy without all those negative messages.

In addition to the happiness traps of money, power, and being fake, there are a few persistent attitudes that are huge obstacles to happiness. These are victimization, feelings of entitlement, waiting for rescue, and blaming. The common thread is staying stuck and focusing on what you can't do, instead of taking full responsibility and control to change your life.

In short, happiness doesn't come from circumstances, and neither does unhappiness. Money, possessions, fame, or power can't make you happy, and terrible things happening to you don't have to make you unhappy unless you hang onto them and let them define you.

The real cause of unhappiness

Unhappiness comes from fear. There are two main fears: the fear of not having enough, and the fear of not being enough.[vi] If you think about it, it makes sense. All the worries about money, job security, possessions, bigger houses, and power come from the fear of not having enough. The worries about what other people think, not being loved, not being able to do something well, or getting fired come from the fear of not being enough.

But why is fear such a huge part of our lives? By world standards, we are incredibly well off, so why are we still afraid of not having enough? And we were obviously good enough to get as far as we are, so why are we still afraid of not being enough? Where does all this fear come from?

The answer is in the structure of the brain. The brain stem, which we share with lizards, is the part with the fight/flight/freeze response. Our ancestors needed this part for the dangerous situations they encountered before we all started building houses and living safe, cushy lives indoors. If a big, hungry animal is after you, you don't have time to ponder, you need the fear instinct to kick in with fight, flee, or freeze, immediately! This reaction is out of place in modern life, when the most dangerous thing most of us face is probably a stapler, but we still have the brain stem looking at everything with fear, because that's what it's built for.

In addition to the brain stem, we also have the amygdala, which we share with other mammals. The amygdala stores all of our bad memories and looks for patterns of things to be afraid of. Again, this was handy when people needed to notice the rustle of grass that meant a tiger was stalking, but not so great in the cubicle farm, especially since the amygdala triggers the endocrine system to release stress hormones like adrenaline and cortisol. You need these hormones if you're running from a tiger, but in modern life, they mostly just make you more likely to have a heart attack.

These two parts of the brain do the fear processing. Basically, they generate unhappiness. Luckily, we don't have let them rule our lives—we have other brain parts that can override them.[vi]

How Happiness Does Work

The ability to be happy comes from the neocortex, the higher brain that is the site of reason, intellect, long-term memory, and the human spirit. This is the part of the brain that has the power to override the fear centers in the brain stem and amygdala and say, "no, calm down, everything is ok." It has the keys to becoming happy.

The way we're wired, it's impossible to concentrate on fear and love at the same time. They're incompatible. So by using the neocortex to focus on love, we can override the fear messages of the lower brain. Specifically, by focusing on appreciation, generosity, personal choice, and simply doing things that are meaningful, we can make ourselves happy. Not a bogus facade of pretend happiness where we go around acting happy even though we're not—real, true happiness.

Chapter 2:
10 Tools for True Happiness

Now that we understand how happiness works, we can use that knowledge to be happier. Studies have shown that the tipping point for being happy is a 3:1 ratio of positive to negative thoughts.[i] That means that when you have fewer than three positive thoughts for each negative thought, nothing much will happen, but once you hit that 3:1 mark, suddenly you will start flourishing.

Notice that the tipping point is 3:1, not 3:0—we're not trying to eliminate negativity altogether or live in some deluded fantasy-land where we pretend bad things never happen, or if they do, they don't bother us. Bad things do happen, and of course they bother us. The goal isn't to become non-human happiness robots. But if we bring in enough positivity to outweigh the negativity by 3:1, we can experience disproportionally great benefits in our lives and start to flourish. These tools and techniques help us get there.

Happiness Tool 1: Gratitude

The fast track to happiness is gratitude. As we saw before, it's impossible for love and fear to co-exist in your brain at the same time. Gratitude is the purest form of love, so it's easiest to access and works the quickest.[x]

One of the fastest ways to be genuinely happier is to develop a gratitude habit. Each night before going to sleep, list five things you're grateful for that day. If you're feeling really low and things are going terribly, sometimes it can be hard to think of five things, but do it anyway. At first it may even be that you're most grateful for things that didn't happen to make things worse; that's all right, too. Just keep at it until you have at least five things.

This is a powerful exercise in a few different ways. First of all, just thinking about things to be grateful for helps you notice the good in your life. Within a few days of starting this habit, you will notice that it gets a lot easier to think of five things to be grateful for, and pretty soon you'll be overflowing your list. I like to insist on a minimum of five things but keep going for as long as I feel like listing things.

As you focus on things you're grateful for, listing them becomes easier because you're training your brain to notice them. Your brain processes zillions of pieces of information every day, and it has to filter out the unimportant stuff, which is most of it. But if you know that later you'll be making a list of things to be grateful for, your brain no longer discards those as unimportant; instead, it notes them. When this happens, suddenly the world seems a lot more positive—you start noticing so many more things to be grateful for.

This also gives you twice as many chances to enjoy the positive experiences of your life: now you're more likely to notice each positive experience and appreciate it as it's happening, and you get to enjoy it again when you think about it for your gratitude list. Furthermore, by focusing on the positive right before going to sleep, you put your mind into a positive mode for the night.[x]

On top of that, positivity attracts more positivity. People are drawn to positivity like plants to the sun, and as you become happier and more positive, people sense it.[xi] Have you ever seen someone so happy, you couldn't help but smile just to watch him or her? Even small things like smiling and saying hello or holding the door for a stranger can make them warm to you and act friendlier.

There are also other gratitude exercises that can put you on the fast track to happiness. Instead of listing any five things that you're grateful, have a theme of the day and list the top five for that: best books, favorite foods, hobbies, treats, people, songs, colors, textures... the possibilities are endless.

If you want to step it up a notch, you can take a few minutes two or three times a day to really savor a small experience. Instead of rushing on, pause and concentrate on enjoying whatever it is: a flower, fall leaves, a dish of ice cream, the sun on your face, an unusual moment of quiet. Or create your own moment by taking time out to think about something that brings you joy. Savoring life's pleasures and sharing them with others is an effective way to increase your happiness.[xi]

Happiness Tool 2: Optimism
The biggest difference between optimists and pessimists is that optimists assume good things are permanent and pervade

every area of their lives, and they assume bad things are temporary and isolated to their limited context. Pessimists do the opposite.[xi]

For most things that happen in life, we'll never know the real reason why they happened, if there even was one, so we might as well use the more positive interpretation when we explain things to ourselves.

For example, say I apply for a job but don't hear back. If I'm an optimist, I'll assume that it's nothing personal and I will get a job eventually, whether this one or a different one. In contrast, if I'm a pessimist, I might start freaking out that nobody wants to hire me because I'm fundamentally flawed, I will never get a job, and nothing will ever get any better.

It's the flip side for positive events. Let's say I enter a picture I took in a photography contest, and win. If I'm an optimist, I will explain it as being a good photographer and having a lot of success in life overall, whereas if I'm a pessimist, I'm more likely to say it was a fluke, or I just got lucky this time.

It seems pretty obvious that the optimistic approach will lead to more positive feelings. But is it foolish to think that way?

I say no. We never learn the true explanation for most situations in life. Was the cashier rude to you because he looks down on you, or because he's having a rotten day? Chances are, you'll never know, but the fact is, people mostly think about themselves and their own issues. If they do something thoughtless, it's probably just that: thoughtlessness. Even in the rare case that someone is trying to hurt you, it's because they're screwed up or suffering in some way—it's still really not about you. It's far more likely the cashier was rude because of something in his own life. Furthermore, you will be happier if you assume his bad manners are due to his own issues. That's two good reasons to assume it has nothing to do with you and move on.

Any time you have a choice, choose to explain good situations to yourself as pervasive and long-term, and bad situations as temporary and isolated. Refuse to take bad things personally. Even if you don't believe these explanations at first, just assume them for the sake of argument, and see how it works out. I'm betting you'll like it enough to stick with it.

Happiness Tool 3: Defeating Faulty Thinking

One of the best things I ever learned about being happier is "don't believe everything you think."[x] We all know that our eyes and ears can deceive us, our hearts don't always have the best judgment, and our hormones can lead us astray. But our thoughts are sacred! We have to listen them because they're the rational part... right?

Not necessarily. Our thoughts are shaped by our assumptions about the world, and sometimes those assumptions are just plain wrong. Our thoughts are also shaped by what we've been in the habit of thinking about in the past. The pathways in your brain become more established each time you go down them, and the ones you don't use fade away. That's why many of us can sing the words to our favorite songs with almost no effort, but hardly remember any world history or trigonometry. Each time you think about something, you're reinforcing that path in your brain.

This means that if you spend a lot of time thinking about the good things in your life, it gets easier and easier to do so, and if you spend a lot of time thinking about the bad things in your life, that gets easier and easier, too.

Also, your interpretation of events may simply be inaccurate. This is especially true if you're in the habit of thinking everything is awful or terrible. If you find yourself thinking something like "I'll never again be as happy as I was when [whatever]," dispute that thought. I don't mean cook up some happy lie to tell yourself, I mean get factual. Do you know for sure that you'll never be that happy again? How do you know? Were you really that happy in the first place? [xv]

Any time you catch yourself feeling down, examine your thoughts. Ask yourself: what am I thinking? Is it really true? Do I know for certain? Is there another way I could look at this that's also true but less painful?

We have great power to make ourselves unhappy with our thoughts. In fact, there are ten common things that people think, that make them miserable and just aren't true.[xv]

Other people's opinion of you is crucial, and if they reject you, it means you're worthless.

There are tons of counter-examples for this. How many great artists and writers never got published or accepted until after their death? There will always be people who think you're great and people who don't. Look for what you can learn from the people who don't, but otherwise, ignore them. If you believe you're doing the right things, that's all that matters. (If you don't, you'll never be happy. Change what you're doing until you do!)

You must not fail at anything important or something terrible will happen.

Fear of failure is a huge roadblock to trying things and doing things. So many of us have the idea that we have to be perfect or nobody will love us and we'll be failures. That is just not true at all. If you suffer from this belief, consider this: are your friends perfect? When they make a mistake, do you hate them and scorn them? That would be ridiculous—they're only human, right? Everybody makes mistakes. *Everybody, including you.* In fact, nothing gets discovered or created without any mistakes. How many times did Thomas Edison try to invent the light bulb before he actually came up with something that worked?

If you refuse to ever fail or make a mistake, you're consigning yourself to a life of passivity, and that's the biggest failure of all. You have to mess up to learn and grow. In fact, sometimes "failures" turn out to be wildly successful and better than the original intent. For example, the removable, re-stickable adhesive that makes Post-It Notes possible was developed in a failed attempt to make a super permanent adhesive.[xvi] We should all be so lucky as to fail like that!

People and things should conform to your idea of the way the world should work. If they don't, they're wrong and bad.

We all have ideas for better ways to run the world—how it *should* be. But the fact is, we don't live in the world of "should," we live in the world of "is." People drive like idiots or maniacs,[xi] they leave their shopping carts blocking the aisle, they litter, they misspell words. You may be able to educate them, but it's unlikely you'll change them. You can only change yourself.

Any time you catch yourself saying "should," notice it. You're wasting energy. No matter how you think things should be, they're not that way, and getting upset about it will not help. Instead, deal with life as it really is.

If something goes wrong, it's somebody's fault. You better make sure it's not yours.

Things go wrong all the time, and finding someone to blame doesn't fix anything. Even if a particular person is clearly responsible for causing the situation, blaming them is unlikely to help. It may make you feel better in the short term, but it hurts the relationship in the long term. (Nobody likes having their nose rubbed in their failings or hearing "I told you so.") Instead, focus on a solution.

Worrying about something will make it turn out better than if you didn't worry.

This is so obviously ludicrous when it's written out, it's laughable, but many of us still act as if it were true. If your worrying points out a risk that you can take action to mitigate, then go for it, but worrying alone helps nothing. Yet we often act like we're falling down on the job if we're not worrying.

If you find it hard to quit cold turkey, this story may help. A. J. Jacobs, editor-at-large at *Esquire* magazine, did a life experiment where he started outsourcing more and more tasks to personal assistants in India. First he had his assistants doing research and clerical tasks, then he had them take over his correspondence. He kept giving them more assignments as he thought of things he didn't like doing. Finally, he realized he was spending a lot of energy worrying about a big project he was working on, and decided to try outsourcing his worry. He didn't outsource the project, just worrying about it. He asked his assistant if she would worry about it in his stead, and she promised: "I will worry about this every day. Do not worry." It worked: "Every time I started to ruminate, I'd remind myself that [my assistant] was already on the case, and I'd relax."ˣ

After I read this, I realized I was worrying about a lot of things, and it wasn't accomplishing anything. I don't have an assistant in India, but A. J. does, and I figured if she's already worrying about his stuff, it's not much more trouble to worry about mine, too. So I decided to pretend to outsource my worrying to her. Every time I felt myself beginning to worry or dwell on something upsetting, I just told myself A. J.'s assistant was on that and I could stop. Nothing came out any worse for my not angsting over it, and I felt a whole lot better. Over time, short-circuiting my worrying this way has become a habit, and I worry much less.

> *Every problem has a perfect solution. Only that solution will do, and you must find it as quickly as possible.*

Most problems have many possible solutions that will work. If you insist that only the perfect one will do, you may spend so much time trying to find it that you can't get started. Meanwhile, the more time passes, the more tempting it is to freak out that the problem isn't solved. It's much more effective to pick a solution and start working toward it. If it turns out there is a better solution, consider switching to it (but make sure the switch doesn't cost more than you gain with the better solution).

Certainly think things through before jumping in, but don't spend so much time analyzing that you never actually get started. What you decide is rarely a permanent commitment—you can change your mind later if it doesn't work out.

It's better to pick one of the many things that will work and get started than to stay paralyzed in your search for the perfect way, or even the best way. A good way is good enough.

It is easier to avoid difficult situations and responsibilities than to face them.

This one is insidious because in the short term, it does feel easier to avoid these things. But over time, the dread associated with these things grows, and the tension of the disconnect between reality and your actions will make you miserable. By avoiding these situations, you're basically pretending they're not there. The bad news and the good news is that reality always wins. Stay away from denial, delusions, pretending, avoiding, or anything that causes a disconnect with reality if you want to be happy.

You can protect yourself from getting hurt by never caring too deeply or investing yourself too much in any pursuit.

So many of us try to stay safe by staying detached. We shoot down ideas because they sound too good to be true, and we don't want to be fooled or taken advantage of. We don't try as hard as we could because then if we fall short, we can always excuse it as not having been our best effort. We don't open up to others for fear of being vulnerable and getting hurt.

This used to be one of my prime directives, and it was extremely scary to try doing things the other way. Admit that I liked that corny movie? People will know I'm not cool! Try something I'm not good at? People might see me fail! Let people see the real me, warts and all? They won't like me! I used to work very hard to keep people from seeing anything but the perfect veneer I presented to them... and then get upset that nobody understood me.

If this sounds familiar, I can tell you from experience, because I've tried it both ways: be real. You may think you're protecting yourself by staying detached, but actually, you still get plenty hurt that way, and you keep yourself from fully living. You can't change the world by shooting other people's ideas down. You can't do something great if you never risk screwing up or letting other people see you being less than perfect. You can't have a truly intimate relationship if you never let another person see the real you, all of you, raw and unvarnished. By staying detached, you keep yourself from ever fully living.

Your past determines your life now and forever.

Nope. Your experiences have shaped who you are, but they only determine your life if you let them define you forever. Don't be a victim, and don't stay mired in your past. Don't use it as an excuse not to be great now. You can't change what happened to you, but you can refuse to give it the power to rule you now.

Bad people and things shouldn't exist, so if they do, you have to get upset about them.

There's that "should" again. Bad people and things do exist. The world is not perfect. People hurt each other, natural disasters and calamities occur, lamentable things happen. But you don't have to get upset about them. It's hard not to sometimes, but getting upset doesn't help anything, so why put yourself through that?

Also, how many times has something happened that wasn't what you were hoping for at all, but looking back, you can see that it all worked out to your advantage? It may help to remind yourself of those times and consider that your current situation may turn out the same in the long run.

Happiness Tool 4: Being Nice to Yourself

Have you ever said "I'm my own worst enemy"? Many of us are, but we don't have to be. By changing what you think, you can be your own best friend instead. Wouldn't that be nice, to have the one person who is always with you helping and supporting you instead of hurting you and making things worse?

You can be your own best friend. Think about what's great about best friends, and be that way to yourself.

Be gentle with yourself. Listen to what you say to yourself, and if you wouldn't stand by and let someone say those things to a close friend of yours, don't stand by while you say them to yourself, either. Think about what you would say to defend your friend, and say it in your own defense instead.

I realize that now you're not only talking to yourself, you're arguing with yourself, but bear with me. If you're already talking to yourself, there are at least two of you in your head. Introducing an extra won't hurt, and may bring you to a pleasant majority!

For example, I used to beat myself up a lot. The first time I tried this, I had just had an ugly conversation with a person who has a long history of being very compelling to me but not very nice. He said some well-targeted things to push my buttons. I ended the conversation promptly and signed off, but I was still upset, and I caught myself thinking "What an asshole he is! I can't believe I've wasted all this time loving him! I'm so stupid! How humiliating!" Normally, I would just go on and on this way, but for the first time, I stopped and listened to what I had said.

"Wait a minute," I thought, "that doesn't even make sense. How does his being a jerk make me stupid? At worst, I was naïve and unrealistically hopeful—is that really so horrible? I acted with love and the best of intentions, and I did nothing wrong. The fact is, I'm going through a pretty hard time and doing the best I can, and I don't need or deserve this kind of harsh judgment."

Hearing these things, even though it was just myself saying them in my head, really helped. It was like a cloud lifted. What the other person said still hurt, but I no longer felt devastated, humiliated, or miserable; more like "gee, that's too bad."

For years I had been my own worst enemy, getting myself into all kinds of stupid situations and causing trouble for myself, and then piling it on by being my own harshest critic and judge. That night, I started being my own best friend instead. It takes a little practice, but it's not that hard, and it really works.

Remember, the first step is recognizing when you're getting into a bogus thought pattern. If you start feeling upset or thinking everything is terrible, awful, never, or always, that's an indicator that you're making yourself upset. That's right, it's not events or other people that make you upset, it's your beliefs about what's going on and your reactions to them. Of course we'd rather good things happen, but how you react when anything happens is up to you. Your feelings come from your thoughts, and we've just seen that your thoughts are not always right. When your thoughts are causing you to freak out, you need to change them.

Once you recognize that you're in a bogus thought pattern, study and dispute it. Ask yourself what thoughts are behind what you're feeling. Then look at each one. Is it true? Do you have proof? How does it make you feel? Is there another interpretation for the situation that's equally true but not upsetting?

In my case, it's often one copy of my voice in my head (Critical Me) attacking another copy (Weak Me): "You never do anything right. Why are you even trying? You'll fail at this, just like you've failed at tons of other things, and everyone will know! You'll be a laughing stock!"

I've found the quickest way to defuse that is to have a third copy of my voice (Advocate Me) stand up to Critical Me, just like I would stand up to someone who was bullying my friend: "Hey, [me] has done plenty of things right! You can't expect to do things perfectly on the first try, but failing is good—it's part of learning, and it's not permanent unless you quit. Maybe there are some mean people who would laugh if this ends poorly, but probably not, and who cares about them even if they do exist? [Me] is an all right sort who's doing the best she can, so lay off."

It sounds ridiculous and crazy, but I've found it very effective. In fact, I hardly ever even need to do it any more. That's partly because my life has settled down quite a bit, but mostly, I just don't think such harsh things about myself any more. By standing up to Critical Me and disputing her thoughts, I've retrained myself to be more accurate and more pleasant in my thoughts. I highly recommend this—my head is a much nicer place to be as a result.

Happiness Tool 5: Responsibility

In order to be happy, we have to take our lives in our own hands. We have to take responsibility for our own happiness, and ultimately, our own destinies. That sounds both obvious and impossible, but in reality, a very small number of people do it. You can be one of them.

It means choosing your present over your past, and your power over the power of anyone else or anything that's ever happened to you. That isn't always easy, and many people never do it for the simple reason that it would change everything. If you, and you alone, control what your life will be from now on, that means you have to act to make it what you want, or accept that you're choosing your current situation voluntarily. A lot of people are too afraid to ever face that, but it is reality.

If you're stuck and want to get unstuck, there are four main ways people give up control of their lives: victimization, entitlement, rescue, and blame.[xx] You need to eliminate these from your life in order to be happy.

Victimization

Have you been wronged? Has something that happened to you kept you from doing what you want to do, or living the life you want?

If so, I'm truly sorry to hear that. I wish the world was the sort of place where things like that didn't happen.

The good news is, you have the power to turn this situation around. Whatever happened, no matter how bad it was, it doesn't have to define your life. It could be your whole story, or it could be just an experience from the past that you've overcome, one of many things that have made you stronger. Only you can choose, and you do have a choice. You can keep holding onto it, or you can let it go. It is standing between you and happiness.

Even if something unspeakably horrible has happened to you, you can still rise above it. Rape victims, children sold into slavery, people who have been blinded or crippled, even Holocaust survivors have managed to overcome the atrocities committed on them and go on to live positive lives.

Consider this quote from *Man's Search for Meaning*, a book by Viktor Frankl about how he and others survived the Holocaust and rose above their time in the concentration camps:

> ❝We who lived in concentration camps can remember the men who walked through the huts comforting others, giving away their last piece of bread. They may have been few in number, but they offer sufficient proof that everything can be taken from a man but one thing: the last of the human freedoms—to choose one's attitude in any given set of circumstances, to choose one's own way.❞ xx

In life's worst circumstances, these people didn't let anyone make them victims. You don't have to either. Starting now, choose to define yourself in a new way, not by what other people do to you or have done in the past, but by what you do. Exercise your freedom to choose your own way.

Entitlement

Entitlement is the idea that someone owes you something. My parents should support me, the government should give me money, my employer should give me a good raise every year, my spouse should make me happy. Notice all the "should"s?

The fact is, the world doesn't owe you a living, and you'll feel better about yourself if you make your own instead. There's much more satisfaction in that.

Rescue

Similar to entitlement, rescue waits for someone else to save you from your current situation. Rescue yourself instead—you have much more control over making it happen, and you won't be obligated to anyone.

Blame

Blame is just a twist on victimization. If you tell yourself you can't be happy because of your wife or your mom or your kids or your boss, or anyone else, you're giving away your power. Other people may have done things to you, and may still be doing them, to add strife, stress, or negativity to your life. That's unfortunate, but it doesn't let you off the hook. You're still choosing to stay in your situation and let it go on as it is.

If you're an able-bodied adult living in a developed country and not in prison, nobody can really make you do anything. Your possibilities are almost limitless. You can get out of almost any situation if you really want to, or you can transform it. It all comes down to you.

If someone is controlling your life, that's only possible because you're allowing them. People will treat you as badly as you let them. If you don't like how someone behaves toward you, you need to renegotiate the relationship or get away from them.

It's comfortable to blame others for your unhappiness, because that way you can feel sorry for yourself safely. Sometimes it feels good to feel sorry for yourself, and you may come to enjoy other people feeling sorry for you, too. Meanwhile, you never have to do anything, because it's all someone else's fault. If you blame others, you're all but guaranteed to enjoy this state forever, because the only way the situation is likely to change is if you act.

I know it's hard—it feels good to be right, and this situation shows that you're clearly right, and someone else is wrong. But think about it, wouldn't you rather be happy than right? Wouldn't you rather *not* be someone to feel sorry for?

Perhaps the hardest part of this is knowing that if you let go of what happened, stop blaming whoever caused it, stop feeling entitled to special consideration because of it, stop being the victim, and stop wanting to be rescued, that means you'll have to make a big change. You'll have to take charge of your own life and decide where to go from here. I know that's really scary! But it's worth it. It's impossible to be happy unless you do.

Here's an example of the alternative. One blogger did a series of posts on bullying and how we as a society need to stop it. In response, thousands of readers have written to him about how they were bullied as kids and it destroyed their self-esteem. He quoted a sampling, all adults writing that they still feel worthless because of the bullying they received in high school.[xxi]

Think about that for a second. Decades ago, some kid said a bunch of mean things...and now, half a lifetime later, those remarks are still defining life for a grown man or woman. How sad and utterly wasteful is that?

Don't be one of those people. Bad things happen, and some people suffer them and go on to live amazing lives, and some people suffer them and go on to be lifelong victims, forever defined by what some asshole said in high school.

It sounds crazy to choose to be unhappy so people will feel sorry for you, but a lot of people do just that. Don't be one of them. You can take charge of your own life and pull yourself up to happiness. Let go of the victimization, entitlement, rescue, and blame. All four of these are just forms of voluntary helplessness. Why be helpless when you can be awesome instead?

Choose to be amazing. It may not be easy, but living a meaningful life isn't. Being happy does require effort on your part, but once you get started, it feeds itself and gets easier and easier.

Happiness Tool 6: Forgiveness

If you really want to be free and powerful, you have to drop your old grievances. That means forgiving.

I won't lie to you, forgiveness can be difficult, especially when someone wronged you in a significant way. On top of that, as a culture, we have a lot of mental blocks on forgiveness.

Forgiving someone doesn't mean you condone their actions. It's easy to think the only way for justice to be served is to refuse to forgive the other person so they keep suffering for their deeds, especially if they haven't even apologized or asked for forgiveness. However, the reality is that the other person's suffering buys you nothing. The harm has already been done.

The crucial thing is to help YOU stop suffering. Ironically, forgiveness is the way to make that happen.[xx]

It doesn't mean you condone what happened or forget it. It doesn't mean you set yourself up for the same thing to happen again later. It just means you release its power over you.

The defining book on forgiveness was written by Everett Worthington and suggests the REACH process:

Recall

Remember the incident as clearly and objectively as you can. Don't think about motives or evil or right vs. wrong, just describe what happened as neutrally and factually as possible. Visualize the event.

Empathize

Try to imagine what the other person's perspective might have been. Imagine if the transgressor was asked to explain him/herself, what he or she might say. Consider that people are most likely to hurt others when they feel attacked or threatened, or when they're afraid, worried, or hurt themselves. They often don't mean to hurt others and don't think about what they're doing; they just lash out in attempt to protect themselves. That doesn't make it right, but it may make it make sense.

Altruistically give forgiveness

Remember a time when you hurt someone but were forgiven. That was a gift. If you can give this gift to your transgressor, it will mean that you are rising above the hurt and anger and being a truly generous person. That is not easy. If you can truly do it from a generous heart, it will set you free.

Commit yourself to this forgiveness
Write a letter to the transgressor, tell your friends, or just write yourself a note—something to make the forgiveness official.

Hold onto forgiveness
You will remember the incident again, and you may feel angry or hurt again when you think of it. Remind yourself that you've forgiven it and move on to thinking about other things.[xx]

* * *

This approach may not work all at once, but I've found it very helpful with things that were hard for me to let go. It may take time and repetition, but you can expunge the bad feeling from your life and set yourself free. You'll be happier and healthier as a result. Remember Viktor Frankl and choose embrace life rather than holding onto grievances.

Happiness Tool 7: Looking for the Good
Another trick that can help speed things along on the journey to happiness is looking for the lesson and the gift in everything. If you look hard enough, you can find something to learn and some good in any situation.

Many events and situations seem terrible at the time, but from our limited view, it's sometimes hard to tell what's bad and what's good. There's a famous Chinese story where a man loses his horse. Everyone says how terrible it is, but he says it could be bad, or it could be good, who can tell? Later, the horse returns with a second horse. Everyone says how great that is, but he says it could be good, or it could be bad, who can tell? His son loves riding the new horse, but falls off and breaks his leg. Everyone says how terrible that is, but he says it could be bad, or it could be good, who can tell? Later, all of the able-bodied young men are drafted to fight a battle, and most of them are killed, but the son can't go because of his broken leg. Everyone says how wonderful that is, but he says it could be good, or it could be bad, who can tell?

We never know how things will turn out, so we might as well assume there is some good in everything that happens. In fact, if we look for something to learn or something to appreciate and find it, then there is some good in it, even if there wasn't before.

In *Happy for no Reason*, Marci Shimoff recommends assuming that the universe is friendly and has your best interests at heart, and everything that happens is for your good.[xx] When I first read this, I thought it was naïve and silly, not to say blatantly untrue, but she recommends trying it for a week. You don't have to believe it for real, just assume it for the sake of argument, the way something is assumed at the beginning of a math proof. Then go about life and see how you feel.

Although I thought it was ridiculous, I tried it anyway. I couldn't believe how much better I felt! The more I looked at things this way—not even from belief, just from exploration of how it could be true—the more it seemed to be true, the more benevolent and nurturing the universe felt to me, and the easier I found it to be happy.

In reality, the universe could be benevolent, malevolent, or neutral, but it almost doesn't matter. If you assume that everything happens for your benefit somehow, and use that assumption to look for the good or something to learn in each situation, then you really do get something good out of every situation. Who wouldn't want that? It's like magic with no magic required.

Happiness Tool 8: Gratifying work

Another thing that builds happiness is doing meaningful work that calls on your strengths. People need a level of challenge that's not so high as to be overwhelmed but not so low as to be bored. If you can find work that requires skill and concentration, is a good match for your key strengths, and provides structure and feedback, you will find it gratifying.[xxv]

Studies have found that it takes 10,000 hours to master a skill.[xxv] That's a lot of time! Generally, the more someone learns and the closer they come to mastery of a skill, the more satisfaction they get from it, and the more interested they become.

Studies on motivation conducted at the University of Rochester found that people do best and enjoy their work most when it meets these three conditions:

- autonomy: being able to manage yourself and control your time

- competence: being good at what you do

- relatedness: a feeling of connection to others[xx]

If you don't already know what you want to do, trying to settle on a passion may take longer than building one by mastering something that meshes well with your strengths. Either way, the important thing to remember is to build up mastery as quickly as possible—being really great at what you do is a form of career capital. Once you have that, use it to get autonomy. Don't just keep working long hours forever in the quest for a better office or more money. Quality of life is much more important.[xx]

But there's more to life than your career; you can find gratifying work in many areas of your life. The best way to do this is by building on your strengths and focusing on work involving them. That's where you'll find the most satisfaction.

If you're not sure what your strengths are, there's a test on the *Authentic Happiness* website (www.authentichappiness.org) called the VIA Strengths Survey. Registration is free, and there are also many other happiness tests there that you can use. This test will help you find your signature strengths. Once you know them, maximize your potential by looking for work that uses them.

It's also important to know what you're trying to accomplish. Do you know what's most important to you? What qualities to you value in yourself? Take the time to list these governing values. When you know them and act in accordance with them, you will feel inner peace; when you stray from them, you will feel uncomfortable.[xx] In fact, if you feel a lot of tension in your life now, there's a good chance your actions are out of sync with your values in some way.

If you're not sure where to start, think about where you spend most of your effort, what you would risk everything for, what you do with your free time, what you would do if you only had six months to live, what you want to be remembered for. These questions can help guide you to your values. Examples of values held by different people include: success, wealth, learning, being a good parent, health, personal responsibility, stewardship, and helping others. Think about your values. List them, write a sentence or two to clarify each one, and prioritize them.

Once you have your values figured out, list your goals. Big and small, what 10 or 15 things do you want to accomplish in the next ten years? Look at how those match up with your values and strengths, and make a rough plan for when you'll work toward them and which one or two you'll tackle first. Get your gratifying work from that—do what it will take to achieve your goals.

As you align yourself with your values and do challenging work that calls on your strengths, you will find yourself absorbed in what you're doing. Sometimes time will pass without your notice, and you won't be aware of yourself or your surroundings, just absorbed in your work. That's called the flow state. You become one with your work. This is the source of deep gratification and great accomplishment. Here's what Mihaly Csikszentmihalyi, who named the flow state, has to say about it:

> ❝It is the full involvement of flow, rather than happiness, that makes for excellence in life. When we are in flow, we are not happy, because to experience happiness we must focus on our inner states, and that would take away attention from the task at hand... Only after the task is completed do we have the leisure to look back on what has happened, and then we are flooded with gratitude for the excellence of that expe-

rience—then, in retrospect, we are happy... The happiness that follows flow is of our own making, and it leads to increasing complexity and growth in consciousness. **99** xxx

You'll never get the flow state by watching tv, but activities like rock climbing, writing, skiing, painting, dancing, or programming are good candidates. For an activity to invoke the flow state, it must:

- require concentration

- be challenging but a good match for your skills

- provide immediate feedback

- represent a harmony between what you feel, want, and think.

It's one of life's ironies that we often choose to spend time passively as a gift to ourselves, when true satisfaction and deep happiness come from doing the things that require more of us.

You can't force the flow state, but you can enable it to happen. Once you've chosen a good flow-inducing activity, the first step is to concentrate on what you're doing. Don't try to multitask—that just keeps you from fully focusing on any of the things you're trying to do. Let yourself be absorbed by one task. If distractions tempt you, acknowledge them but direct yourself back into your work. If you think of something else that you really want to research or need to remember to do, make yourself a little note and go back to what you're doing. xxx

This may be difficult at first. We're a society of quick changes and constant interruptions. But you can get in shape for it just like building muscles by exercising. To start, plan to work for 20 minutes straight, then take a 10-minute break. Knowing a break is coming as a reward is very helpful in the beginning, and committing to stick with your task for 20 minutes is also crucial. Set a timer for 20 minutes or write down your start time, and don't stop until time is up. You may encounter many distractions and temptations. The worst obstacle may be that you really don't want to do the task or it seems scary or overwhelming. Keep telling yourself it's only 20 minutes, then you'll get a break. Keep working until then.

When the time is up, feel the satisfaction of having stuck with it. Reward yourself with a break, and notice how much progress you made. Twenty minutes isn't long, but it's surprising how much you can accomplish in that time if you focus.

As you keep repeating this process, it gets easier and easier. Especially, for me, the hardest part of a task is starting. Once I've spent one or two blocks of 20 minutes on it, I get some traction and have a much easier time. If you're stuck at the beginning, another thing that helps is using some of your first 20-minute block to make a plan of attack and start breaking the task down. As you reduce it to smaller and smaller pieces, it becomes more concrete. You start to see how you could do each piece, and it becomes less daunting.

As you keep working in 20-minute increments, you may find that the timer goes off right when you're in the middle of something and you actually don't want to stop. Awesome! Keep going! Give yourself a break when you do get tired or reach a good stopping point.

As you develop the ability to get absorbed and work on your project for longer stretches, you may actually find the timer counter-productive if it startles you out of your flow state and back into awareness of the world and time passing. If you find that's the case for you, instead of using a timer, just record the start time of each session. If you're longing for a break, look at the clock and direct yourself back into the task until 20 minutes is up, but if you're flowing away at the task, you won't be interrupted by the timer.

Try to eliminate or minimize other sources of interruption, too. Anything that forces you to surface from the flow state is the enemy of your gratifying work. If you're working on something really serious or important, it's worth turning off the phone, putting a note on your door, and definitely turning off the email auto-notification. If it's urgent, people will find a way to get your attention, but otherwise, they can wait until your break.

Gratifying work that takes you to the flow state is a great source of true, deep happiness. The satisfaction of accomplishing things feels good, and the flow state is downright addictive. If you can combine that with doing something you love, it's an abundant and reliable source of happiness that's available any time you want it.

Happiness Tool 9: Giving

Remember, love leaves no room for fear in your brain. True giving from the heart is an expression of love. It's also an expression of gratitude—out of the fullness of what you have, you spread good to someone else.

Giving feels good, and it creates positive feelings in recipients, too. They feel gratitude and warmth, which they reflect back to you and radiate out into the world. It starts a contagious upward spiral of positivity. It also makes you feel one with the universe. Whereas simple pleasures and having fun fade, doing good for someone else has a more lasting effect.

That's the awesome part of giving. It's very powerful for increasing your happiness and positivity.

It only works if it's true giving from the heart, though. A lot of people make the mistake of thinking they're giving when they do something out of a sense of obligation, or do something they don't want to do for someone else as a "sacrifice." In fact, I used to think those were the only gifts that counted— that if I wasn't suffering some in the giving, it was really a gift to myself, not a gift to the other person. If you think this, let me tell you, you've got it all backwards.

True giving flows from love. It feels good and brings joy to you as well as the recipient. They're intermingled. When you do something you feel obligated to do or resent doing, that isn't love. The true motivation there is fear or guilt—or both.[xxx] Think of examples from your own life, and I'll bet you'll see it's true. The things you do for others that you resent or don't like doing, you probably do for one of these reasons:

- You're afraid the other person will be angry or won't like you if you don't

- You're afraid God will be angry if you don't

- You're afraid something bad will happen if you don't

- ❧ You're afraid people will think you're a bad person if you don't

- ❧ You think you'll be a bad person if you don't

- ❧ The person you're doing something for has done a lot for you in the past, so you'd feel guilty if you didn't do this for them

None of those has anything to do with love—they're all fear and guilt. Fear and guilt are not love, and they can't co-exist with it.

Gifts given out of fear or guilt aren't gifts at all, not just because love isn't involved, but also because the recipients can tell. No matter how hard you try to put on a smiling face, people can sense your tension or resentment. You're not fooling anyone. Your negative energy taints the whole transaction. The flow of love that should occur when someone gives doesn't happen, because the transaction isn't based on love in the first place, and everybody feels negativity as a result.

If you talk to the other person involved, you may be surprised to find that they didn't even want what you were doing in the first place. This came as quite a shock to me: many of the things I hated most weren't even things the other people wanted or cared about. No wonder they never acted grateful! What an incredible waste of energy!

On top of that, studies have shown that faked positivity is every bit as stressful and dangerous for your body, particularly your cardiovascular system, as anger.[xx] So stop!

Unless you can do something out of a true desire to do it,

with a heart full of love, don't do it. This may mean you have to take a break from some of your usual activities for awhile, maybe even avoid some people or situations altogether. It's that important—do it.

Meanwhile, take some time to figure out how you got into those situations in the first place. Often, when people give resentfully or with the expectation of something in return, it's because they don't like themselves and don't feel worthy of love. If you think nobody will like you for yourself, maybe they would like you if you did nice things for them. Maybe they'd even start to depend on you, and then they'd have to like you because they needed you.

If you recognize this in yourself, face the truth: you can't buy people's love that way. But you don't need to. You are worthy of love just for being you. Look for the good in yourself and nurture yourself. That is the source of strength; once you get to that point, you will have love in your heart to overflow in gifts to other people.

Another way to check whether your gift is a true gift is to examine your motives. Before you give the gift, consider what you're expecting to happen as a result. If you will be hurt or angry if the other person doesn't send a thank you note or gush about your gift, it's not a true gift, it's an obligation. True gifts are satisfying and complete unto themselves. That doesn't mean it wouldn't be polite and courteous of the other person to acknowledge your gift with gratitude—it certainly would. But you can't control what someone else does, you can only control what you do. If you expect something in return, again, it's not a gift. In this case, it's more of a request, so why not just be direct and ask for attention? See if the other person would like to get together for coffee or talk. You may find that afterward, you feel so good, you can truly give the gift out of love; in that case, feel free to do it!

Giving true gifts requires a certain amount of strength. If you dwell in fear, you don't have love to give. Keep shifting yourself from the fear mode to love by practicing gratitude and the other exercises mentioned above. You can also take a shortcut by starting with very tiny gifts. Try to put yourself in the other person's place and feel compassion for him or her, then step in with a smile. For example, if you see someone carrying a lot of stuff toward a building, it's easy to think of a time when you've had a lot of things to carry and how nice it would have been to have some help. Then smile and open the door for him or her. It costs you nothing but makes a big difference to the person carrying the boxes! Often, the person will smile and thank you, and a warm feeling will pass between you. Even if not, though, remember how difficult it is to carry so many things, assume the person is in a big hurry to put it all down and would have thanked you if his or her arms didn't hurt so much, and continue feeling good about doing something nice.

Doing tiny acts of kindness like opening the door for someone is an excellent way to start an upward spiral of positivity. (Another good one is letting the person with only two things go ahead in the checkout line.) Actions like this are so small, they cost you almost nothing, so you don't need a big reserve of love to draw from, yet they often mean so much to the recipient, they can leave you both feeling good all day. As you stop doing the things you resent and build a habit of giving these tiny gifts when you can, you will find that your love and positivity grow. You can build up to doing bigger and bigger things out of the overflowing love in your heart. Just let it happen naturally—don't push yourself. Instead, do things when you feel a pull of desire to do them. This will keep you drawing from love and increasing your capacity over time.

You can give best of all when you combine your passions and strengths with a cause you care about. The power of multiple sources of positive energy will cause a contagious upward spiral that will effect people around you and build through you. That is something to strive for.

Happiness Tool 10: Balance

Another aspect that enables happiness is balance. It's hard to be sustainably happy when you're neglecting any of the three key areas of your life: health, relationships, and purpose. Try to do something toward each of these every day, even if it's small.[xxx]

Health

We hear tons of messages all the time telling us to eat more fruit and vegetables, and less fat and refined carbohydrates. Yet most of us don't do it. Fatty, sugary, salty, chemical-filled processed food is abundant and effortless in the short term, but it really does make you feel worse. I think another factor contributing to this problem is that factory-farmed food is so bland and tasteless, so if you can convince yourself to eat unprocessed chicken or veggies, you're rewarded with a flavorless, bland meal of blah that makes it all the easier to get the McNuggets next time.

If you really want to feel better, I urge you to try eating locally grown fresh food. If you eat meat, get pasture-raised chickens and beef.[xxx] Get your eggs from pasture-raised chickens. Look for milk that hasn't been ultra-pasteurized or homogenized. Then cook your own meals from these natural foods. It's amazing how much better they taste than the grocery store equivalents. (Even the ones in the grocery store that say "free range" or "organic" are almost certainly factory farmed and will not have as much flavor or nutrition). Go to the farmer's market or deal directly with local farmers for as much of your food as you can. You'll be improving your own life as far as nutrition and taste, and you'll also be improving the farmers' lives and the animals' lives.[xxxv] A lot of people try to buy the cheapest food, but what you eat makes a huge difference in how much energy you have. It's worth investing in yourself—get the best.

We also need to move. Even at a cellular level, movement stimulates growth and renewal; a sedentary life causes decay.[xxx] Exercise also releases happy chemicals in the brain, which makes it a great mood lifter when you're blue for no reason. For optimal mood improvement, aim for 30-45 minutes of exercise a day. More than an hour or less than half an hour is not as good for mood.[x] Exercise also increases blood flow to your brain and helps you think and remember things better.[xl] In particular, studies have shown that getting outside and being in nature improves positivity and broadens the mind.[xl] A nice walk in the woods is a great way to combine the benefits of nature with the benefits of exercise, plus it's a good opportunity to gather your thoughts.

Another thing we often neglect in our busy modern lives is sleep. It is almost impossible to be happy when you're sleep deprived! Everything seems so much bigger, more dramatic, and more insurmountable. Studies have shown that sleep deprived people are considerably impaired in their functioning, and after only a few days of missing a few hours' sleep, our bodies stop being able to process sugar properly and become insulin-resistant. That leads to cravings, spikes and crashes in blood sugar, and storing a lot of fat in the belly, right where we don't want it.[xli]

If you want to enjoy your life, you must get enough sleep. Make it a priority. For anyone who doesn't have trouble falling asleep, get to bed by 10. Marci Shimoff calls this "catching the 10:00 angel train,"[xl] and it's made a huge difference in my life. For people who just toss and turn if they go to bed early, I recommend reading *The Power of Rest: Why Sleep Alone Is Not Enough. A 30-Day Plan to Reset Your Body* by Matthew Edlund.

Relationships

Even the most introverted among us need connections with other people. Take the time to keep in touch with your friends and family, and feed those relationships. It's important to have those connections when you're down and need help, but it's also important to have them when you're happy. Sharing your joy, laughter, and gratitude increase them in you, help them spread, and strengthen your relationships. That's a win all around.

Purpose

Spend at least a little time each day on your meaningful work. This will give you gratification and satisfaction. It's your chance to be fully yourself and make your mark on the world.

Overcoming obstacles to balance

By incorporating health, relationships, and purpose into every day, you make sure to keep yourself fed and thriving, so you can keep getting better and better, and happier and happier.

Taking care of yourself is a commitment. When you think about tending your health, relationships, and purpose every day, do you feel anxious about when you'll find the time? Most of us are overtaxed and stressed, scheduled to the max and rushed during most of our time. That, too, is an obstacle to happiness.

The problem with life is that it's finite. You can't do everything—it's impossible. A lot of us act as if this isn't the case, but it is.

If you can't do everything, some things have to go. You'll never get to them. Shouldn't those be the things that are less important?

A lot of us don't really consider the relative importance of the things we do, we just do whatever is most urgent, or whatever is easiest, or whatever somebody has nagged us about most recently. But the fact is, many of the urgent or easy tasks are really not that important. If you want time to take care of yourself, build your relationships, and do meaningful work, you may have to cut out some things that are less important. That's what it takes to improve your life.

When looking for things to cut, some prime areas are meetings, web surfing, email, and television. These four activities are huge time wasters for many people. A more systematic approach is what I call the to-quit list. If you're like most people, you probably have a long list of things you're supposed to do, either in your head, on a piece of paper, in a computer file, or on a flurry of Post-It notes stuck everywhere. Gather the whole list together in one place and give it a good, hard look. How many of those things give you a feeling of dread or aversion when you think about them? Start a new list called your "to-quit list" and put all those things on it.

Of course, if you quit everything on the list right now, there will probably be some pretty bad consequences. It's tempting to say "I can't just quit my job!" or "I can't quit the X committee—the whole thing would fall apart!" But the fact is, it's not a matter of "can't." What if you were in an accident that landed you in the hospital for a month, and you couldn't do anything? You wouldn't be doing any of the things on your to-do list, yet the world would not end. Someone else would take care of the crucial things. Some important things might not get done, and a lot of unimportant things wouldn't get done, but the world would keep turning and you wouldn't die, at least not from missing a meeting or failing to wax your car.

The reality is that you *can* quit anything you want. If you stick with something, it's because you see some value in it, you don't want to deal with the consequences of quitting, or you just haven't thought it through. For example, many people hate their jobs and think they can't quit. The fact is, you *can* quit your job... but then you'll have to find another source of income and/or find a way to need far less money. Another option is to keep your job but see if you can negotiate an alternate work schedule to free up some time for yourself. If you can work from home some days, you can save the time you would have spent commuting. Another possibility is working less than full-time. I've cut back to 80% of full-time at my job, and it's amazing how great it is having those eight hours of my life back each week! If you really hate your job, though, work on getting a new job or a new source of income to replace it. Life is too short to waste so much of it being miserable.

Similarly, if you find that your relationship with a certain person is a big source of dread or angst, ask yourself why you are in this relationship. What are you getting out of it? Is there a way to change it so that you can be happy in it? If not, quit! For as difficult or ugly as it may be in the short term, in the long term, you both deserve to be with people who can facilitate your happiness.

Those are the two biggies; compared to work and relationships, quitting a boring club or an officer position in a group is a piece of cake! These things can be hard, too, but put them in perspective: if you moved away or were stricken with serious medical problems, someone else would take over the tasks you do. If these tasks aren't bringing your joy or meaning, they're taking away from something more important you could be doing. I'm not saying you need to be rude or leave people in the lurch, but give them notice, offer to train your successor, and move on.

As you work on your to-quit list, it's also important to keep new things from getting added to it. Saying no can be hard, but it's a lot easier than quitting later! When people ask you to take on new responsibilities, make "no" your default answer. If you really enjoy doing something or it contributes to your most important values, you can always change to a "yes" later.

Conclusion

You can have a good life by doing work that involves your signature strengths every day, feeding your relationships, and taking care of yourself. To have a meaningful life, take it a step farther and put your efforts toward something that advances knowledge (learning, teaching, science, writing), power (technology, engineering, building or making things), or goodness (police, firefighter, or any kind of service).

No matter what your circumstances, you have the power to make yourself happier. Live your life according to your values, take action to make your life what you want it to be, and use the happiness tools.

Remember that a 3:1 positivity ratio is the key to flourishing, so grow in positivity and share with everyone. Be your best self. The world needs you!

Want More?

If you liked this ebook or found it valuable, please pass it on! Share it with anyone who might benefit from it. Also, I write about happiness and other related topics on my blog at http://17000-days.com. Check it out—I'd love to have you!

If you want to go deeper, check out *Getting Unstuck*, my next book about transforming your life. You might also enjoy my inspirational coloring book for adults. It's called *Relax and Color*. It combines many of the premises in this book with intricate, beautiful pictures to color.

How to be Happy is the first book I wrote. I put this book together because it's the best information I've found about enjoying life. I think it's sad that so few people in this world are happy, when we all have the power to change that with the right information. Just imagine if everyone started being more positive and doing things they loved! Not only would those people be happier and doing great things, but there would be fewer fearful, insecure, unhappy people around to be mean and cause problems. Let's spread the word!

Resources

Many excellent books have been written on this subject. These are the ones I've found most helpful:

What Happy People Know by Dan Baker and Cameron Stauth. Rodale, Emmaus, PA, 2003.

If you read only one book on improving your life, I recommend choosing this one. It contains all the bits and pieces I've spent a few years gathering from other sources and putting together in my mind. It puts them all together in a tidy, easy-to-understand package that is an enjoyable and uplifting read.

Authentic Happiness by Martin Seligman. Free Press, New York, NY, 2002.

Learned Optimism by Martin Seligman. Vintage, New York, NY, 2006.

Martin Seligman is one of the founders of the field of positive psychology. His research focuses on what makes people thrive, as opposed to psychology's traditional focus on pathology. His books are informative and focused on helpful suggestions and self-evaluation.

Positivity by Barbara Fredrickson. Crown Publishers, New York, NY, 2009.

This is a very detailed book on the same sort of happiness described in this ebook, only the author calls it "positivity" instead of "happiness" to distinguish it from the superficial feel-good self-help kind. She gets very detailed and cites tons of scholarly research, her own and others. If you're looking for a rigorous treatment of the subject, this one's for you.

Happy for no reason by Marci Shimoff. Free Press, New York, NY, 2008.

This one is less grounded in science and strays a little into affirmation and magic, but it is still a very good handbook on changes you can make in your life to increase your everyday level of happiness.

How to keep people from pushing your buttons by Albert Ellis and Arthur Lange. Birch Lane Press, New York, NY, 1994.

This is an excellent reference on the Activating Event -> Beliefs -> Feelings and Behavior model of behavioral theory, which basically says that it's not events or other people's actions that cause your feelings or behavior, it's your beliefs about those events. Thus, you can control how you feel and react. The writing style is a little crusty, but the information is gold.

Notes

iBaker, Dan, and Cameron Stauth. What Happy People Know. Rodale, 2003, p. 19.

iiShimoff, Marci, with Carol Kline. Happy for no reason. Free Press, New York, 2008, p. 18.

iiiibid., 27.

ivibid., 39

vBrickman P, Coates D, Janoff-Bulman R. "Lottery winners and accident victims: is happiness relative?" J Pers Soc Psychol. 1978 Aug; 36(8):917-27.

viFredrickson, Barbara. Positivity. Crown Publishers, New York, 2009, p. 35.

viiBaker, Dan, and Cameron Stauth.. What Happy People Know. Rodale, 2003, p. 24.

viiiIbid., p. 27; Shimoff, Marci, with Carol Kline. Happy for no reason. Free Press, New York, 2008, p. 88.

ixFredrickson, Barbara. Positivity. Crown Publishers, New York, 2009, p. 35. See also Fredrickson, B. L., R. A. Mancuso, et al. "The undoing effect of positive emotions," Motivation and Emotion 24 (2000): 237-58 and Fredrickson, B. L., and R. W. Levenson. "Positive emotions speed recovery from the cardiovascular sequelae of negative emotions." Cognition and Emotion 12 (1998): 191-220.

xBaker, Dan, and Cameron Stauth.. What Happy People Know. Rodale, 2003, p. 81.

xiShimoff, Marci, with Carol Kline. Happy for no reason. Free Press, New York, 2008, p. 131.

xiiFredrickson, Barbara. Positivity. Crown Publishers, New York, 2009, p. 55.

xiiiSeligman, Martin. Authentic Happiness. Free Press, New York, 2002, p. 107; Fredrickson, Barbara. Positivity. Crown Publishers, New York, 2009, p. 183.

xivSeligman, Martin. Authentic Happiness. Free Press, New York, 2002, p. 88.

xvShimoff, Marci, with Carol Kline. Happy for no reason. Free Press, New York, 2008, p. 84.

xviIbid.

xviiEllis, Albert, and Arthur Lange. How to keep people from pushing your buttons. Birch Lane Press, New York, 1994, p. 63.

xviii Time-Life Books. Library of Curious and Unusual Facts: Inventive Genius. Time-Life Education, Virginia, 1991, p. 73. Cited on http://www.snopes.com/business/origins/post-it.asp

xixCarlin, George. Napalm and Silly Putty. Hyperion, New York, 2001. p. 5.

xxFerriss, Timothy. The 4-Hour Workweek. Crown Publishers, New York, 2007, p. 117.

xxiBaker, Dan, and Cameron Stauth. What Happy People Know. Rodale, 2003, p. 148.

xxiiShimoff, Marci, with Carol Kline. Happy for no reason. Free Press, New York, 2008, p. 52.

xxiiiDan Pearce. "Less Talk. More Walk." Single Dad Laughing. http://www.danoah.com/2010/10/are-we-all-talk-or-are-we-going-to-fix.html

xxivSeligman, Martin. Authentic Happiness. Free Press, New York, 2002, p. 75; Shimoff, Marci, with Carol Kline. Happy for no reason. Free Press, New York, 2008, p. 133.

xxvSeligman, Martin. Authentic Happiness. Free Press, New York, 2002, p. 79.

xxviShimoff, Marci, with Carol Kline. Happy for no reason. Free Press, New York, 2008, p. 40.

xxviiSeligman, Martin. Authentic Happiness. Free Press, New York, 2002, p. 176.

xxviiiGladwell, Malcolm. Outliers: The story of success. Little, Brown, and Company, New York, 2008.

xxixDeci, Edward, and Richard Ryan. "About the theory." Self-Determination Theory. http://www.psych.rochester.edu/SDT/theory.php

xxxNewport, Cal. "Beyond Passion: the science of loving what you do." Study Hacks. http://calnewport.com/blog/2010/01/23/beyond-passion-the-science-of-loving-what-you-do/

xxxiCsikszentmihalyi, Mihaly. Finding Flow. Basic Books, New York, 1997, p. 32.

xxxiiFiore, Neil. The Now Habit. Tarcher/Putnam, New York, 1989, p. 137.

xxxiiiCloud, Henry, and John Townsend. Boundaries. Zondervan, Grand Rapids, MI, 1992, p. 91.

xxxivFredrickson, Barbara. Positivity. Crown Publishers, New York, 2009, p. 35. See also Rosenberg, E. L., P. Ekman, et al. "Linkages between facial expressions of anger and transient myocardial ischemia in men with coronary artery disease." Emotion 1 (2001): 107-15. and Moskowitz, J. T., and E. S. Epel. "Benefit finding and diurnal cortisol slope in maternal caregivers: A moderating role for positive emotions." Journal of Positive Psychology 1 (2006): 83-91.

xxxvBaker, Dan, and Cameron Stauth. What Happy People Know. Rodale, 2003, p. 226.

xxxviRobinson, Jo. ""Health benefits of grass-fed products." Eat Wild. http://www.eatwild.com/healthbenefits.htm

xxxviiGRACE. "The Issues: Introduction." Sustainable Table. http://www.sustainabletable.org/issues/

xxxviiiFredrickson, Barbara. Positivity. Crown Publishers, New York, 2009, p. 75.

xxxixBaker, Dan, and Cameron Stauth. What Happy People Know. Rodale, 2003, p. 238.

xlThe Franklin Institute. "The Human Brain."

http://www.fi.edu/learn/brain/exercise.html#physicalexercise

xliFredrickson, Barbara. Positivity. Crown Publishers, New York, 2009, p. 193; see also Marc G. Berman, John Jonides, and Stephen Kaplan. "The Cognitive Benefits of Interacting With Nature." Psychological Science, vol. 19 (2008), no. 12, pp. 1207-1212.

xliiSpiegel, Karine, Rachel Leproult, Eve Van Cauter. "Impact of sleep debt on metabolic and endocrine function." The Lancet, 354:9188 (October 23, 1999), pp. 1435 – 1439.

xliiiShimoff, Marci, with Carol Kline. Happy for no reason. Free Press, New York, 2008, p. 174.

Made in the USA
Lexington, KY
01 August 2016